The Boston Post Road
was one of the first roads
in America.

Although we think of the Boston Post Road
as one road, it has always been,
in fact, three separate roads.
The roads connect New York City
and Boston, Massachusetts.

New York City

BY GAIL GIBBONS
FROM PATH TO HIGHWAY

Upper Post Road

(The Northern Route)

About 250 miles long. This is the road that the first postrider traveled.

Springfield

Middle Post Road

About 225 miles long. This is the shortest of the three roads.

Hartford

Lower Post Road

(The Southern Route)

About 270 miles long. This became the most frequently traveled of the three roads.

New Haven

Boston

Dedham

Providence

Newport

Thomas Y. Crowell · New York

The Story of the Boston Post Road

Special thanks to Myrna D'Alessandri of the Bronx
County Historical Society, The Bronx, N.Y.; John
Cushing of The Massachusetts Historical Society,
Boston, Mass.; Philip L. Forstall of Rand McNally &
Co., Chicago, Ill.; Ruth Pepin of The Vermont
Department of Libraries, Montpelier, Vt.

From Path to Highway:
The Story of the Boston Post Road
Copyright © 1986 by Gail Gibbons

Library of Congress Cataloging in Publication Data
Gibbons, Gail.
   From path to highway.

   Summary: A history of the Boston Post Road to the
present day.
   1. Post-roads—New England—History—Juvenile
literature.   2. Post-roads—New York (State)—History—
Juvenile literature.   3. New England—Description and
travel—Juvenile literature.   4. New York (State)—
Description and travel—Juvenile literature.
I. Title.   II. Title: Boston Post Road.
HE356.AllG53 1986   388.1'0974   85-47897
ISBN 0-690-04513-1
ISBN 0-690-04514-X (lib. bdg.)

First Edition   1 2 3 4 5 6 7 8 9 10

About 500 years ago . . .

Snap!

A branch breaks. Indians make their way through the forest, following a narrow path.

They walk the same trails their Indian ancestors walked. Over hundreds of years moccasined feet have worn smooth paths between villages and hunting grounds.

Clomp . . . clomp . . . clomp . . .

It is 1640. The paths are now trod by the heavy boots of Colonists, people new to the land.

The Colonists use the Indian paths to travel between their separate settlements. The paths become more deeply worn.

Clip clop . . . clip clop . . .

A new sound is heard on the forest paths—horses! The horses have been brought from England for the growing colonies. Men on foot, riders on horseback—many use the narrow Indian paths now. The paths become wider.

The year is 1673. A lone horseman gallops along the path. This rider is on an important mission for his Governor. He is the first person to carry mail—"the post"—in this country. He is the "postrider."

He hurries along the northern trail from New York City to Boston. At times the path is hard to follow and he must hack his way through wilderness. He has instructions to watch for river crossings and resting spots for other postriders who will later use the trail.

It takes the postrider fourteen days
to reach Boston. He then returns to
New York City with mail from Boston in
his saddlebags. The entire journey takes
four weeks.

Clip clop . . . clip clop . . .

Clip clop . . . clip clop . . .

It's 1704. A brave woman, Sarah Knight, is traveling from Boston to New York City on the southern trail. She travels with a postrider as her guide.

Boston

New York City

It is a long, rough journey. When she arrives back in Boston she scratches into a pane of glass with her ring:

Now I've returned to Sarah Knight's
Thro' many toils and many frights
Over great rocks and many stones
God has presarv'd from fracter'd bones.

By the 1700s the colonial settlements have grown into small villages. Now carts and wagons move along the paths with their heavy loads. The paths have become roads.

Chink . . . chink . . . chink . . .

The Post Roads are becoming known. Now it's 1753 and Benjamin Franklin, newly appointed Deputy Postmaster for the Colonies, is requiring that postage be paid for every mile the mail must be carried. Milestones, to mark the miles, are driven into the ground. The roads are much wider now.

Something new is seen on the roads—
stagecoaches. In 1772, the first stagecoach
in service makes the trip between Boston
and New York City in just one week.
Although the passengers ride inside a
coach, the journey is still a hard one—
bumpy and tiring.

Now it is 1775. The Revolutionary War begins. The American Colonists fight for their independence from England. The Post Roads must be used for maneuvering soldiers and equipment to places of battle. All stagecoach service stops. The mail can't go through.

1785. The war has been over for a few years. Travelers are on the road again. The Post Roads are important links between the states of the new American nation. Sections of the roadbed are strengthened. There are roadbeds made with logs—corduroy roads—or with planks.

The Post Roads keep changing. Bridges are built to replace the old ferry crossings. Farmers and tradesmen add gravel and stone to the sections of the roadbed that they own. They install tollgates—wooden pikes that block the road. When the traveler pays the toll at the tollgate, the gatekeeper turns the pike to let him through. He continues his journey on the "turnpike."

Whoa . . .

The roads are busier than ever now. Inns have been built along the way as stopping places for weary travelers.

There is comfort at the inn. You can get a hot meal, a bath, and a bed for the night.

One inn guest, Mr. Shenstone, wrote:
Whoe'er has travelled life's dull round,
Where'er his stages may have been,
May sigh to think that he has found,
His warmest welcome at the inn.

Refreshed, the travelers are ready for whatever the next leg of their journey may bring.

Chug . . . chug . . . chug . . .

A train—an "iron horse"—rounds the bend. It is 1850. A train now connects Boston and New York City, and passengers can make the trip faster than ever before.

Parts of the southern road have been taken over for the train's trackbed. Horses and wagons now travel alongside the train—the road has been moved over.

The train carries a lot of passengers and goods that used to go by road. The road is quiet . . . but not for long.

BREAD

Honk! Toot!

It's 1920 and the road is busy again. The automobile is here. The southern route is now the most frequently traveled of the old Post Roads.

The roadway is smooth. Sections are paved with concrete to bear the heavy weight of cars and trucks.

Stores and businesses line the roadside.

Varoom . . .

Today the Boston Post Road is crowded with cars, trucks, and buses. In some places the road winds through countryside . . .

and in other places it cuts through towns and cities. There are more stores, more businesses . . . motels, service stations, fast food stops . . . billboards and flashing lights.

Today it takes less than a day to travel between New York City and Boston. The narrow Indian path . . .

has become a modern four-lane highway.
In the years to come, the Boston Post Road
will no doubt change again.

Famous Travelers of the Boston Post Road

Paul Revere sped along the Boston Post Road to carry news of the Boston Tea Party to New York.

George Washington frequently traveled the Post Road, staying overnight at inns along the way. Some of those inns are still standing, marked with plaques that read "George Washington slept here."

Sarah Knight, that early traveler of the southern Post Road, was Benjamin Franklin's schoolteacher in Boston!

As Deputy Postmaster, **Ben Franklin** had milestones installed along the road. Some people jokingly called them "Franklinstones."

Henry Wadsworth Longfellow often traveled the northern route, staying at an inn called Howe's Red Horse Tavern. Longfellow wrote a book about the inn called *Tales of a Wayside Inn.* In it were these well-known lines: "Listen, my children, and you shall hear/Of the midnight ride of Paul Revere." The book made Howe's Red Horse Tavern famous overnight. The owner officially changed the name of his establishment to Wayside Inn.

Mark Twain's books *The Adventures of Huckleberry Finn* and *The Adventures of Tom Sawyer* were based on his memories of a boyhood spent in a Mississippi River town. But as an adult Twain lived in Connecticut, and frequently used the Boston Post Road.